Level A

Writing
— for —
Proficiency

A Test Preparation Program

GLOBE FEARON
EDUCATIONAL PUBLISHER
PARAMUS, NEW JERSEY

Paramount Publishing

Executive Editor: Barbara Levadi
Editorial Developer: Curriculum Concepts, Inc.
Production Director: Penny Gibson
Manufacturing Supervisor: Della Smith
Senior Production Editor: Linda Greenberg
Production Editor: Alan Dalgleish
Marketing Manager: Sandra Hutchison
Electronic Interior Design: Curriculum Concepts, Inc.
Art Director: Nancy Sharkey
Cover Design: BB&K Design Inc.

Printed in the United States of America
3 4 5 6 7 8 9 10   99 98 97 96

ISBN: 0-835-90890-9

GLOBE FEARON
EDUCATIONAL PUBLISHER
PARAMUS, NEW JERSEY

Paramount Publishing

CONTENTS

Introduction

Unit 1: Writing For the Essay Test

Chapter 1: The Three Elements of Good Writing

Chapter 2: Four Types of Essays

Unit 2: Improving Your Score

Chapter 1: Planning Your Essay

Chapter 2: Strategies for Clear and Interesting Writing

Chapter 3: Mechanics and Usage

Chapter 4: Revising and Proofreading

Unit 3: Preparing to Take the Writing Test

The Business Letter

SUCCEEDING ON THE WRITING TEST

Soon you'll be taking your state's writing test. So will many other students in the state. There are three big questions that students wonder about as they prepare for the test. This book is going to answer those questions.

THREE BIG QUESTIONS

1. What's Going to Be on the Test?

- You're going to be asked to write an essay. Most tests will give a written assignment called a **prompt**. Here's an example of a prompt you might be asked to respond to:

> *The principal in your school wants to start a dress code. This dress code would require boys to wear jackets and ties two days a week. Girls would have to wear dresses or skirts. Do you agree or disagree?*

- The test may also include questions and will give you a choice of answers. This is a **multiple-choice test**. Here's an example of a multiple-choice question:

Direction: The word underlined below may be correct or incorrect. Choose the letter next to the correct form of the word.

The car that Becky is driving is <u>hers</u>.

- Ⓐ hers
- Ⓑ her's
- Ⓒ hers'
- Ⓓ hers's

This book will give you many opportunities to write essays. You'll learn what a good essay is all about. And you'll get a chance to practice some strategies that will help you write a successful essay based on your own good ideas. You'll also learn about multiple-choice tests and strategies to help you do well on them.

2. How Am I Going to Be Graded?

A reader will score your writing test. That reader is specially trained to evaluate your writing. Here are some points the reader will look for in your essay.

- Does the essay answer the prompt clearly and completely?

- Is the writing clear and to the point?

- Is the essay well organized?

- Does the essay give reasons that support its ideas?

- Does the essay contain good grammar, spelling, and punctuation?

This book will help you learn what you need to know to answer "Yes!" to all of these questions. You'll learn how to plan and write a well-organized essay. You'll also learn how to tell if you have written one.

3. What Do I Have to Do to Get a Good Grade?

The answer to this question is BE PREPARED! These ideas will help you.

- Practice writing as much and as often as you can. The more you write, the better you'll become at writing.

- Learn how to recognize and correct your mistakes.

- Have confidence in yourself. You have good ideas. You can learn how to write about those ideas.

- Learn how much time you can give to each part of the test.

You will see this clock on some pages of this book. It is there to remind you that most writing tests will be timed. The time on the clock is to give you an idea of how much time you would have if you were taking the test.

Now it's time for you to begin making sure that you succeed on your writing test. Remember, you can do it!

U N I T 1

WRITING FOR THE ESSAY TEST

What Is An Essay?

An **essay** is a short piece of writing. You write an essay to say what you think about a topic.

The person who grades your essay will expect to find four things:

1. The **central idea**: the most important idea of the essay. Your whole essay will be about this idea.

2. The **introduction**: the first paragraph of the essay. Give the central idea in a sentence at the beginning of the introduction.

3. The **body**: the middle part of the essay. The body should be two or three paragraphs. Each paragraph should contain one thought about the central idea.

4. The **closing**: the last paragraph. In the closing, state the central idea again. You can use different words, but be sure the meaning is the same.

Here is a picture to help you remember the parts of an essay.

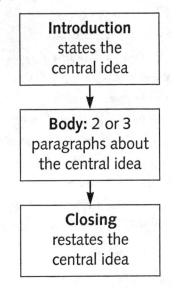

Introduction
states the
central idea

↓

Body: 2 or 3
paragraphs about
the central idea

↓

Closing
restates the
central idea

CHAPTER 1 — THE THREE ELEMENTS OF GOOD WRITING

Knowing and using these three keys to good writing will help you get a better grade on your writing test:

- **Focus** Everything in your essay should be about your central idea.
- **Support** Give details to back up your central idea.
- **Organization** Start with the central idea. Give details. Then repeat the central idea in your closing paragraph.

LESSON 1 — A Good Essay

Read the prompt below. Then read the essay.

Check It Out

> *The principal in your school wants to start a dress code. This dress code would require boys to wear jackets and ties two days a week. Girls would have to wear dresses or skirts. Do you agree or disagree?*

Our principal wants to start a dress code in our school. I	1
think this is a very bad idea.	2
Kids should be free to decide how they look. Junior high	3
students need to practice making good decisions. How can we	4
practice if the school makes every little decision for us?	5
A dress code is unfair to kids who don't have formal clothes.	6
A dress code will make these students feel bad twice a week.	7
They'll feel that they don't measure up. A rule that makes people	8
feel bad about themselves is bad.	9
Also, dressy clothes make it hard to relax. Kids must be	10
relaxed to do good work. For example, I can't keep my mind on	11
homework if I'm uncomfortable. That's why I work in comfort-	12
able clothes. I know I'll do my best work that way.	13
A dress code will make students unhappy and uncomfortable.	14
It definitely won't help us make decisions for ourselves.	15

Work It Out

Look back at the essay. Here are some examples of how the writer uses focus, support, and organization.

Focus

- In lines 1-2 of the essay, the writer answers the prompt with the central idea. The central idea is that a dress code is a bad idea.

- Every sentence in the essay is about the writer's opinion that a dress code is a bad idea.

Support

- The writer supports the central idea with details. Details can be facts, reasons, or examples.

- The writer gives three reasons.
  (1) Students should be able to decide how they look.
  (2) A dress code is unfair to kids without formal clothes.
  (3) Formal clothes make it hard to relax.

- The writer then gives details to support each reason. For example, in lines 8-10 the writer tells why a dress code is unfair to kids without formal clothes. The reason is that a dress code will make them feel bad twice a week.

Organization

- The writer organizes the essay so that the reader can follow its ideas easily.

- The writer states the central idea in the first paragraph.

- The writer gives three details to support the central idea in the next three paragraphs.

- The writer restates the central idea in the last paragraph.

Look It Over

This lesson tells about the three elements of good writing. Is focus, support, or organization the hardest part of essay writing for you? Explain why.

_____

_____

_____

_____

_____

Focus Your Writing

Once you decide on your central idea, stick to it. You might come up with other interesting thoughts. However, use only the thoughts that are about your central idea. Doing this helps you **focus** your writing.

Check It Out

Below is a writing prompt and an essay. Some sentences in the essay are not about the central idea. Can you find these sentences? After you read the prompt and essay, answer the questions that follow.

> *Tell why one thing you own is very important to you. What makes it so special?*

When I was eight, my uncle gave me a baseball glove for my   1
birthday. Since that day, it's been the favorite thing I own. That   2
glove makes me feel like a real baseball player. I'll never forget   3
the first time I wore it. I want to be a major league player some-   4
day. I know it's hard to make it as a pro, but I am going to give it   5
my best shot. If you really put your heart into it, you can make   6
your dreams come true.   7

I wear my glove every time I play. I am ready when a ball   8
comes my way. Usually I am the shortstop, but I can play out-   9
field, too. Sometimes I'm the catcher, but I like playing in the   10
infield or outfield better.   11

Anyway, my glove helps me feel like a good player. I guess   12
you could say it is like an old friend. I consider my baseball   13
glove the best thing I own.   14

Work It Out

1. The central idea is stated in line 3. Copy it here.

    _____

    _____

    _____

2. What thoughts about the central idea does the writer include in lines 8-11?

    _____

    _____

    _____

3. Which sentences in lines 8-11 are **not** about the central idea?

_____

_____

_____

_____

4. Which sentences in lines 12-14 are **not** about the central idea?

_____

_____

_____

_____

5. What words does the writer use to repeat the central idea in lines 12-14?

_____

_____

_____

_____

Look It Over

How could you make this essay more focused on the central idea? Which sentences would you take out? Write one new sentence for the essay that relates to the central idea.

_____

_____

_____

_____

_____

_____

_____

_____

_____

A good essay has lots of details about the central idea. Here are three different kinds of details you can use:

- **facts:** details that can be proven
- **examples:** details that give more information
- **reasons:** details that tell why or how

Details make your central idea easier to understand and more interesting.

Check It Out

Read this prompt and essay. The essay needs more details to back up the central idea. As you read, think about where you would add them. Then answer the questions that follow.

> *What makes you especially angry? Why do these things make you angry?*

There are lots of things to be angry about in the world.	1
I guess what makes me really angry is when people are mean	2
to each other.	3
One thing that makes me feel really angry is seeing kids	4
ganging up on someone. They did this last month when a new	5
student came to school. Instead of being friendly, most people	6
didn't talk to him. A couple of really mean people picked on him	7
because he is from a foreign country. My brother and I were	8
the only ones who were friendly.	9
I also get angry when adults don't trust me.	10
My sister often gets me angry because she borrows things	11
without asking.	12
Many people get angry for different reasons. But the mean	13
things people do to each other get me really angry.	14

Work It Out

1. What is the central idea of this essay?

   _____

   _____

2. What thought does the writer discuss in lines 4-9?

   _____

   _____

3. What details in lines 4-9 help you understand the writer's central idea?

_____

_____

_____

4. Are the details in lines 4-9 facts, examples, or reasons? What other details would you include?

_____

_____

_____

5. Does the writer use details in line 10? What details would you add to support the central idea?

_____

_____

_____

6. What details would you add to lines 11-12?

_____

_____

_____

Look It Over

What do you think is the most important idea to remember about adding support to an essay? Explain your reasons.

_____

_____

_____

_____

_____

_____

_____

_____

Organize Your Writing

When you write an essay, you will need to put your ideas and thoughts in some kind of order. In other words, you have to organize them.

If you are asked to describe your home, you can organize your ideas by writing about one room at a time. You can start with your favorite and end with your least favorite. You can organize the details you give about each room. Give the most important detail first and the least important detail last.

Check It Out

Read the prompt and essay below. As you read, think about whether the writer organizes her reasons well. Then answer the questions that follow.

> *What is the most important thing you own?*
> *Why is it special?*

Every day I wear my gold locket. I never take it off, even when	1
I'm sleeping. It's the most important thing I own.	2
My locket is beautiful. It is oval. It has flowers engraved on	3
the front. When you open it, there is space for two photos. I love	4
to look at it and the photos inside.	5
My grandmother gave me the locket. She got it from her	6
mother, so it is very old. I feel important because Grandma	7
wanted me to have it. Nobody has anything like it, not my	8
friends or even my mother. This is probably the most important	9
reason why I love my locket so much.	10
The locket also reminds me of my twelfth birthday last	11
summer when I got it as a present. My whole family went to	12
Puerto Rico to see Grandma. I was small the last time I saw her,	13
and I missed her very much. Whenever I look at the locket,	14
I remember that trip.	15
For all these reasons, this locket is the most special thing	16
I own. I will give it to my daughter someday.	17

Work It Out

1. What is the central idea of this essay?

_____

_____

_____

2. What four reasons does the writer give to support the central idea? Write the reasons in order as they appear in the essay. Then number the reasons according to how important you think they are. Make **1** the most important and **4** the least important.

_____

_____

_____

_____

3. Explain why putting the reasons in this order would make the essay better.

_____

_____

_____

_____

4. Suppose the writer had lost her locket. How would you change the organization of the essay to include that detail?

_____

_____

_____

_____

Look It Over

Write yourself a tip for organizing an essay that uses several reasons to support the central idea.

_____

_____

_____

_____

_____

_____

_____

Put Your Learning into Practice

You have learned that in a good essay, the writer states the central idea in the introduction. You have also learned that each paragraph in the body includes a thought about the central idea. In the closing the writer restates the central idea. Use what you have learned to complete this page.

Check It Out

Read the prompt and essay. Then answer the questions that follow.

> In many towns and cities, people recycle items they have used at home, work, and school. Choose one item and discuss why it should be recycled.

People should recycle paper instead of wasting it.   1

Often junk mail and school exercise papers get thrown away.   2
But the clean side of those sheets of paper could be written on.   3
Also, grocery bags can be used again. People throw away paper   4
bags all the time. When bags get thrown out, more trees have   5
to be cut down.   6

People could save money by using paper again.   7

An important reason to recycle paper is to save trees. Forests   8
are cut down all the time. Air gets more polluted because trees   9
put oxygen in the air. The air gets worse all the time, especially   10
in the city. We really need more trees in the city.   11

Also, if people recycle more paper, less of it will be burned in   12
incinerators. The air will be less polluted with smoke.   13

It would be better if people thought about recycling paper   14
instead of wasting it.   15

Work It Out

1. What is the central idea of the essay?

   _____

   _____

2. What thoughts about the central idea does the writer include?

   _____

   _____

   _____

3. What details does the writer include about the central idea?

_____

_____

_____

_____

4. In lines 8-12, what sentences are **not** focused on the central idea?

_____

_____

_____

_____

5. The writer repeats some thoughts in more than one place. Tell why reorganizing these sentences would improve the essay.

_____

_____

_____

_____

Look It Over

Write yourself a tip to help you remember how to improve the focus, organization, and support of an essay.

_____

_____

_____

_____

_____

_____

_____

_____

_____

CHAPTER 2

FOUR TYPES OF ESSAYS

This chapter tells you about four types of essays that are on most writing tests. The essays are **persuasive**, **descriptive**, **expository**, and **narrative**.

LESSON 1

What Are the Different Types of Essays?

PERSUASIVE ESSAY

In a **persuasive essay**, you give your opinion about a problem or an idea and try to make the reader agree with your opinion.

The prompt

The prompt in a writing test may ask for your opinion about a problem or idea. You will be asked to back up your opinion with reasons, examples, and facts.

Words to look for in the prompt

- agree
- disagree
- opinion
- idea

Who should decide which subjects are taught in school—students or teachers? Write an essay that gives your opinion on this issue.

Your goal

To give an opinion and make a reader agree with it.

The plan

- Read the prompt. Underline the important words and ideas in the prompt.
- Decide what you think about the topic. What is your opinion?
- List all the **reasons** for your opinion.
- List **examples** and **facts** that back up your opinion.

DESCRIPTIVE ESSAY

In a **descriptive essay**, you describe a person, place, or thing.

The prompt

The prompt in a writing test might ask you to describe your favorite relative or your neighborhood.

Words to look for in the prompt

- describe
- see
- smell
- detail
- hear
- taste
- touch

> *Describe your favorite place and tell why you like being there.*

Your goal

- To give the reader a clear idea of what you're describing.
- To help the reader experience what you're describing.

The plan

- Read the prompt, and decide what you want to describe.
- Think about the special parts of what you are going to describe. Put them into a sentence. For example, "My neighborhood is a busy, noisy place."
- Close your eyes and visualize what you are describing.
- Think of details that describe the person, place, or thing you're writing about. The details should help the reader see, hear, smell, feel, or taste what you're writing about.
- Use words that give details. For example, don't call a smell *bad* or *great*. Instead, use words such as *bitter* or *flowery*.
- If you're describing a place, you can use words such as *above*, *below*, and *behind*.
- You can sometimes make a description real for a reader by comparing what you are describing to something else.

Think It Over

What do you think you will find most difficult about writing a descriptive essay? Write your ideas on a separate sheet of paper.

EXPOSITORY ESSAY

In an **expository essay**, you explain something or give information about a topic.

The prompt

The prompt might ask you to discuss a problem in your community. It might ask you to explain how to play your favorite video game or to define what something means to you.

Words to look for in the prompt

- explain
- tell how
- problem
- define
- discuss
- process

> *Tell about a problem in your community.*
> *Give examples that show why it is a problem.*
> *How would you solve this problem?*

Your goal

To explain or give information about something to a reader.

The plan

- Read the prompt. Decide what it's asking you to write about. Underline important words and phrases in the prompt.

- Choose a topic you know something about. If the prompt asks you to discuss a problem in your town, write about a problem you've thought about before.

- Think about your solution to the problem. Give reasons why your solution is likely to solve the problem. If you can, give examples of how this kind of solution has worked in the past.

- Consider why the problem was caused in the first place. If you analyze the causes of a problem, it will often help you find a solution.

- If you're explaining how to do something, use words such as *first*, *next*, *then*, and *finally*.

- Use details to make your essay clear for a reader.

Think It Over

On a separate sheet of paper, write about how you will remember the most important parts of an expository essay.

NARRATIVE ESSAY

In a narrative essay, you tell a story. The story can be real or made up.

The prompt

The prompt might ask you to tell about something that happened to you in real life. It might ask you to make up a story that teaches an important lesson.

Words to look for in the prompt

- relate
- tell about
- characters
- experience
- events
- real life
- setting
- story
- situation

> *Tell about a time when you felt very afraid. What frightened you? How did you handle the situation?*

Your goal

To tell a story, either a real one or one you make up.

The plan

- Read the prompt, and decide if you're going to write about something that really happened or about something made up.

- Give details that will help the reader "see" where the story takes place.

- Tell **where** and **when** the events take place. Describe the characters in your story, and tell what they say.

- Include details that will describe how the characters look, speak, and feel.

- Describe the events in time order. What happens first? What happens next? What happens last?

- If you want your essay to teach a lesson, think about what lesson you want to teach. Do the events in your essay really teach the lesson?

Think It Over

How is a narrative essay like a movie or TV program? Write your thoughts on a separate sheet of paper.

How to Write a Persuasive Essay

Here's a prompt that might appear on a writing test.

> *Who should decide which subjects are taught in school—students or teachers? Write an essay that gives your opinion on this issue.*

You can plan a persuasive essay by comparing the two sides of the issue. After deciding on your opinion, you can list the reasons for and against your opinion in a chart.

Your essay can argue for the reasons in the first column and against the reasons in the second column.

Opinion: Students should decide which subjects are taught.	
Reasons for: Students would be interested in school and not drop out.	**Reasons against:** Sometimes uninteresting subjects are important.
Students would choose subjects that are important to them.	Students might only study things that are easy.
Students wouldn't act up in class because they would like school.	

Compare the chart with these paragraphs from a persuasive essay.

> Students should be able to choose the subjects they study in school. Though some people may think students would only study easy subjects, I don't think this is true. Kids aren't lazy.
>
> Teachers don't always know what every student wants to learn about. But the kids themselves know what's important to them. Every student has some subjects that are interesting and some that aren't very interesting. If students could pick their favorite subjects, they might feel that school is more interesting and not drop out.

Look back at the essay. Circle the central idea. Underline details from the chart that the writer uses in these two paragraphs.

Plan a Persuasive Essay

Now it's your turn to plan a persuasive essay. Read the prompt below.

> *Who should decide which subjects are taught in school—students or teachers? Write an essay that gives your opinion on this issue.*

Start Out

Think carefully about the issue. Do you agree or disagree? Jot down your reasons.

5 MIN

_____

_____

_____

_____

_____

Now look at your reasons. Use them to write your opinion in a sentence.

_____

_____

_____

Think of some examples and facts that will support your opinion. Think of your own experiences and your friends' experiences. Also think about anything you've heard, seen, or read about the topic.

Example 1:_____

_____

_____

_____

_____

Example 2:_____

_____

_____

_____

_____

Put It Together

You've stated your opinion and found some reasons and examples to support it. Now you can make your own chart to plan your essay. Here are some ideas to help you.

- Be sure that you answer the prompt.
- Check to see that each of your reasons and examples backs up your opinion. You can add more reasons and examples if you think they're important.
- Arrange your reasons in order of importance. Put the most important first and the least important last.

Fill in the chart with your opinion, reasons, and examples.

Your Opinion: _____

_____

_____

Reason 1: _____

_____

_____

Example: _____

_____

_____

_____

_____

Reason 2: _____

_____

_____

Example: _____

_____

_____

_____

_____

Write Your Essay

Now you're ready to write your persuasive essay. Use the notes from your chart as you write.

- State your opinion in the first paragraph.

- Then put your reasons in order. Put the most important reason first and the least important reason last.

- Write a short paragraph for each reason. Include at least one detail to support each reason.

- Finish your essay with a closing paragraph that restates your opinion one last time.

Write your essay on a separate sheet of paper.

Look It Over

When you've finished writing, read your essay carefully. Use this checklist to evaluate your work. For now, don't worry about spelling or grammar.

Circle a number on the scoring scale after each question. (**5** is the highest you can score; **1** is the lowest.)

Do you clearly state your opinion about the issue in the first paragraph?   1   2   3   4   5

Does your second paragraph give one reason and at least one example?   1   2   3   4   5

Does your third paragraph give one reason and at least one example?   1   2   3   4   5

Do you give your reasons and your opinion again in the closing paragraph?   1   2   3   4   5

Think It Over

If you had to write this essay again, how would you change it? Write your ideas on the lines below.

_____

_____

_____

_____

_____

How to Write a Descriptive Essay

Here's a prompt for a descriptive essay that you might find on a writing test.

> *Describe your favorite place and tell why you like being there.*

In a descriptive essay, you use details to help your reader see, hear, smell, feel, or taste what you're describing. You can also describe your feelings about your topic. One way to plan your description is to make a **detail web**. Look at the example.

TOPIC: My favorite place

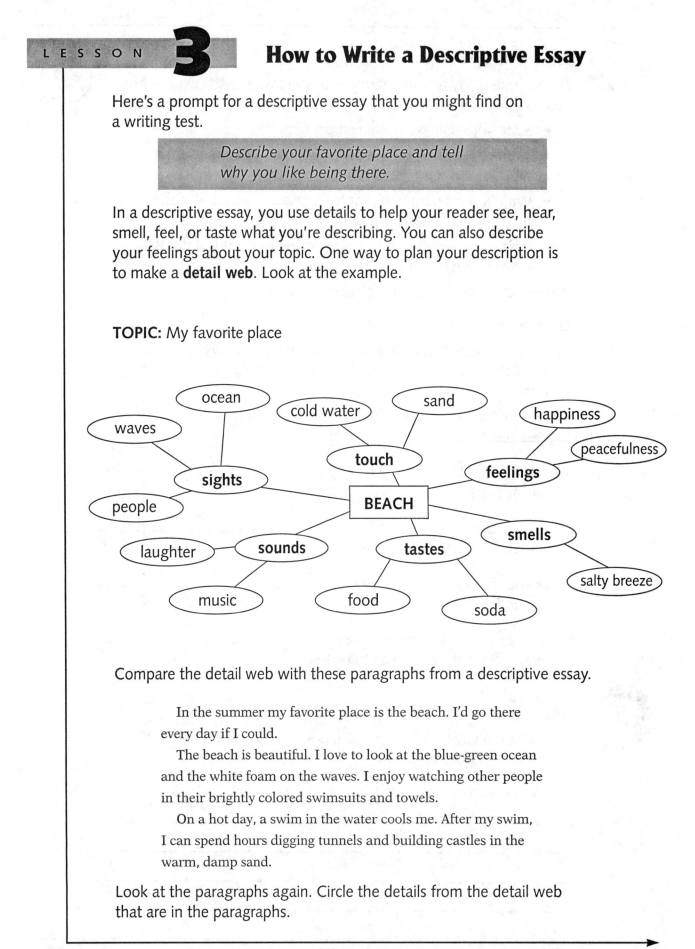

Compare the detail web with these paragraphs from a descriptive essay.

> In the summer my favorite place is the beach. I'd go there every day if I could.
>
> The beach is beautiful. I love to look at the blue-green ocean and the white foam on the waves. I enjoy watching other people in their brightly colored swimsuits and towels.
>
> On a hot day, a swim in the water cools me. After my swim, I can spend hours digging tunnels and building castles in the warm, damp sand.

Look at the paragraphs again. Circle the details from the detail web that are in the paragraphs.

Plan a Descriptive Essay

Now it's your turn to plan a descriptive essay. Use the prompt below.

> *Describe your favorite place and tell why you like being there.*

Start Out

Use what you know. Think of places you've been. This list may give you some ideas. Add ideas of your own.

- What's the most beautiful place you've ever seen?

_____

_____

- Where do you go to have fun?

_____

_____

- What places bring back happy memories?

_____

_____

_____

_____

Choose the place you want to describe. List everything you like about the place.

_____

_____

_____

_____

_____

_____

_____

Write a sentence that tells how your favorite place makes you feel. This will be the central idea of your descriptive essay.

_____

_____

_____

Put It Together

You already have your topic and central idea. Now you can use the detail web to come up with details to use in your essay. Here are some questions to help you.

- What different kinds of things do I see when I'm at my favorite place?

- What are some noises I hear when I'm there?

- Do I smell anything, such as food or flowers?

- Do I have any other feelings besides the one I stated in my central idea?

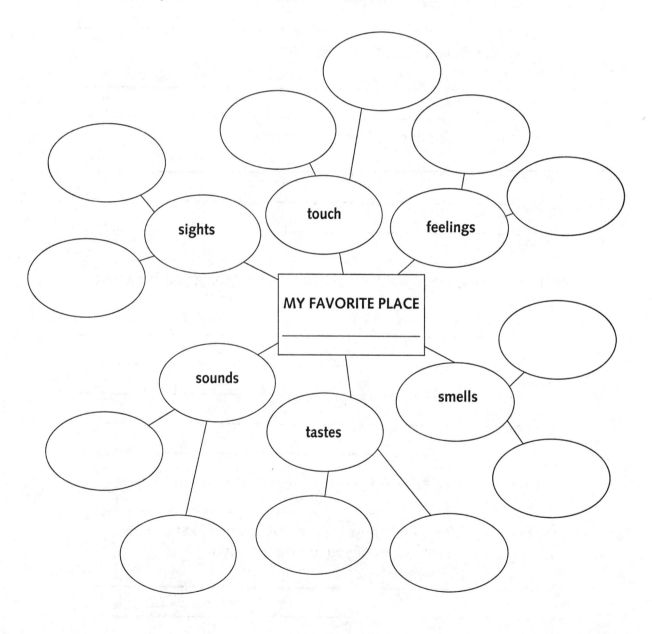

25 MIN

Write Your Essay

Now you're ready to write your descriptive essay. Use your detail web to help you.

- Remember to tell in your first paragraph what your favorite place is and how you feel about it.
- Put details from your detail map in groups that make sense together.
- Write about each group of details in a separate paragraph.
- Finish your essay with a closing paragraph that tells again why you like to be in your favorite place.

Write your essay on a separate sheet of paper.

Look It Over

When you've finished writing, read your essay carefully. Use this checklist to evaluate your work. For now, don't worry about spelling or grammar.

Circle a number on the scoring scale after each question. (**5** is the highest you can score; **1** is the lowest.)

Do you name your favorite place in the first paragraph?

1   2   3   4   5

Do you tell why it is your favorite place?

1   2   3   4   5

Do you include details to help your reader picture the place?

1   2   3   4   5

Does your closing paragraph name your favorite place again?

1   2   3   4   5

Think It Over

If you had to give a friend 3 tips about writing a descriptive essay, what would your tips be?

_____

_____

_____

_____

_____

How to Write an Expository Essay

Here's a prompt for an expository essay that you might find on a writing test.

> *Tell about a problem in your community.*
> *Give examples that show why it is a problem.*
> *How would you solve this problem?*

This prompt asks you to explain a problem and give a solution. One way to plan an expository essay is to make a **table of problems and solutions.** Look at this table.

TOPIC: Drunk driving is a problem in our town; it can be solved.

PROBLEMS	SOLUTIONS
People get killed in alcohol-related accidents.	Don't ride with a drunk driver.
Pedestrians get run over.	Be careful crossing streets.
Some people drive drunk again and again.	Drunk drivers must be punished.

Compare the table with this expository essay.

Drunk driving is a big problem in the cities and small towns of this country. It is also a big problem in our town.

Each year, several people are killed and injured by drunk drivers. Last summer, a drunk high school boy crashed his car into a tree beside the high school. His girlfriend, who was sitting next to him, died instantly. She was only seventeen. My best friend's ten-year-old cousin was killed while crossing the road to his house. He was hit by a drunk driver who didn't see him.

We can do several things to protect ourselves. First of all, we shouldn't get in a car if the driver has been drinking. We should also be careful crossing streets. Most importantly, when we become drivers, we should never drink and drive.

Though drunk driving is a serious problem, it can be solved.

Look back at the essay. Underline the problems the writer mentioned. Circle the solutions.

Plan an Expository Essay

Now it's your turn to plan an expository essay.

> *Tell about a problem in your community.*
> *Give examples that show why it is a problem.*
> *How would you solve this problem?*

Start Out

Choose a problem that you know about from experience, from talking to others, from reading newspapers, or from television shows. Look at the list below for ideas. Add some ideas of your own.

Problems: drugs, crime, homelessness, unemployment, racism

- _____
- _____
- _____

Once you've decided on a topic, think about how the problem affects your community. Jot down ideas as you think of them.

_____
_____
_____
_____
_____
_____

What is the most serious aspect of this problem?

_____
_____
_____
_____

Your choice of the most serious aspect of the problem can be the central idea of your essay. Write a single clear sentence that gives your central idea.

_____
_____
_____

Put It Together

Now that you have chosen a problem to write about, you can use the table of problems and solutions to plan your essay. Here are some ideas to help you.

Look back over the ideas you jotted down on the last page. You can probably use some of them in your table of problems and solutions.

Topic: _____

Central idea: _____

PROBLEMS	SOLUTIONS

Write Your Essay

Now you're ready to write your expository essay. Use your table of problems and solutions to write the body of your essay. These ideas will help you.

- State the problem in your first paragraph. Also state the most important point or central idea about the topic.
- Write a paragraph about other issues related to the main problem you're writing about. Give examples.
- Write a paragraph that offers solutions to the problems.
- Finish your essay by stating your main idea one last time. You can also leave the reader with a strong reminder about the seriousness of the problem.

Write your essay on a separate sheet of paper.

Look It Over

When you've finished writing, read your essay carefully. Use this checklist to evaluate your work. For now, don't worry about spelling or grammar.

Circle a number on the scoring scale after each question. (**5** is the highest you can score; **1** is the lowest.)

Question	1	2	3	4	5
Do you clearly state the problem in the first paragraph?	1	2	3	4	5
Do you describe accurately how the problem affects your community?	1	2	3	4	5
Do you use real-life examples?	1	2	3	4	5
Do you offer solutions to the problem?	1	2	3	4	5
Do you finish with a strong statement that wraps up your essay?	1	2	3	4	5

Think It Over

If you were going to write a review of your essay, what would you say?

_____

_____

_____

_____

How to Write a Narrative Essay

Here's a prompt for a narrative essay that you might find on a writing test.

> *Describe a time when you felt very afraid.*
> *What frightened you? How did you handle*
> *the situation? What did you learn from it?*

A narrative can be about something that really happened, or it can be a story that you make up. A **story map** can help you plan a narrative essay.

TOPIC: A time when I felt afraid

Central Idea: I was afraid of having a tooth pulled because I thought it would be painful.

Details: Nervousness before dentist appointment
My mother tells me ways to deal with fear.
I follow her plan and it works.

Conclusion: There are ways to conquer your fears.

Compare the story map with this narrative essay.

> When the dentist told me that he would have to pull a tooth, I thought I would die! I was afraid it would be painful. But I learned how to use my imagination to conquer my fears.
>
> I was really nervous the night before the appointment. Then my mother gave me some advice. She said that when the dentist was working on my tooth, I should close my eyes and picture myself having fun with my friends.
>
> That's exactly what I did. I imagined I was at the park playing basketball with my friends. I was enjoying my daydream so much I hardly felt my tooth being pulled.
>
> Now that I know how to conquer my fear, I don't think I'll be afraid of visits to the dentist.

Look back at the essay. Underline the details from the story map.

Plan a Narrative Essay

Now it's your turn to plan a narrative essay.

> *Describe a time when you felt very afraid.*
> *What frightened you? How did you handle*
> *the situation? What did you learn from it?*

Start Out

5 MIN

To help you get started, think about your own experiences. The list below has some ideas you can use. Add some ideas of your own.

- Have you ever had to talk in front of people?

  _____

- Have you ever had to try something you've never done before?

  _____

- Have you ever heard a strange noise at night?

  _____

  _____

Now choose one incident to write about. Then jot down some notes about your experience.

WHERE _____

_____

WHEN _____

_____

WHAT HAPPENED _____

_____

_____

HOW I HANDLED THE SITUATION _____

_____

_____

WHAT I LEARNED FROM THE EXPERIENCE _____

_____

_____

What you learned from the experience is your central idea.

Put It Together

Now that you know what you want to write about, you can use a story map to finish your plan. The ideas you wrote down on the last page will help you complete the map.

5 MIN

TOPIC: _____

_____

Central Idea: _____

_____

_____

_____

_____

_____

Details: _____

_____

_____

_____

_____

_____

Conclusion: _____

_____

_____

_____

_____

_____

_____

_____

Write Your Essay

Now you're ready to write your narrative essay. Use your story map. These ideas will help you.

- Put the events in the order in which they happened.
- Use details to describe how you felt at different times during your story.
- Your conclusion could describe your relief when you found that there was nothing to be afraid of. If you write your story well, the reader will feel relief, too!

Write your essay on a separate sheet of paper.

Look It Over

When you've finished writing, read your essay carefully. Use this checklist to evaluate how well you did. For now, don't worry about spelling or grammar.

Circle a number on the scoring scale after each question. (**5** is the highest you can score; **1** is the lowest.)

Does your first paragraph tell what the story will be about?

1   2   3   4   5

Do you describe your feelings throughout the story?

1   2   3   4   5

Do you tell the events in the order in which they happened?

1   2   3   4   5

Does your closing paragraph tell what you learned from the events?

1   2   3   4   5

Think It Over

Look back at your essay. Is there anything you would add or leave out? Explain why.

_____

_____

_____

_____

_____

_____

Use this outline to write your thoughts about the meaning of each of the key points in Unit 1. Don't worry about writing complete sentences.

A. Parts of an Essay

1. Central Idea _____

_____

2. Introduction _____

_____

3. Body _____

_____

4. Closing _____

_____

B. Three Elements of Good Writing

1. Focus_____

_____

2. Support_____

_____

3. Organization _____

_____

C. Four Kinds of Essays

1. Persuasive_____

_____

2. Descriptive _____

_____

3. Expository_____

_____

4. Narrative_____

_____

IMPROVING YOUR SCORE

What Can You Do to Be a Better Writer?

In this unit, you'll learn how to put your thoughts in order when you write. You'll also learn how to write correct sentences and how to use capital letters and punctuation marks. The unit tells you how to find and correct misspelled words and other mistakes.

When you finish this unit, you'll know:

- how to think of something to write about after you read a prompt
- how to put your ideas into sentences and paragraphs
- how to make your writing clearer
- how to correct misspelled words and other mistakes.

This diagram shows steps you can take to improve an essay before, during and after you write.

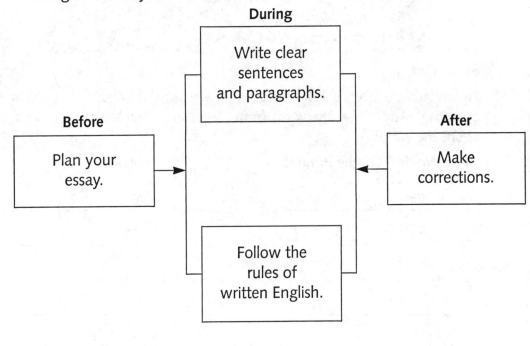

During

Write clear sentences and paragraphs.

Before

Plan your essay.

After

Make corrections.

Follow the rules of written English.

CHAPTER 1 PLANNING YOUR ESSAY

You'll probably get a better grade if you plan your essay carefully before you write it. In this chapter, you'll learn how to use the prompt to get ideas, how to limit your topic so that you can finish in the time allowed, and how to develop and order your ideas.

LESSON 1 How to Think of Ideas

"I'm usually not good on tests. I get nervous and my mind goes blank. I have ideas, but I can't think of them." — **Louisa Calkins, 13**

Some people "freeze" on tests and can't get started. If this happens to you, try these strategies:

- Take a deep breath, and relax. Find the key words in the prompt.

- Use the key words to help you think of a topic and ideas.

Here's a prompt that you might find in a writing test.

> *Many people think that certain kinds of guns should be illegal. Do you agree or disagree? Write an essay that gives your opinion. Remember to support your opinion with reasons, examples, and facts.*

Start Out

Two words are listed below. Beside each key word is an idea that might go with it. Add other key words from this prompt. Write your ideas about the words.

Key Words from the Prompt	Ideas
guns	dangerous
illegal	could get arrested

2

How to Extend an Idea

"I can think of topics to write about, but sometimes I can't think of enough ideas about the topic to write a whole essay." —**Tad Mather, 12**

Do you ever have trouble thinking of enough ideas and details for an essay? When you do, try these strategies:

- Write down everything you know about the topic. You can write sentences, phrases, or just words. Don't worry about order. This kind of thinking and writing is called **brainstorming**.

- Write any words that come to mind about the topic. This is called **freewriting**. You might find more ideas this way.

Here's a prompt you might find on a writing test.

> *Tell about the most exciting event that has hap-*
> *pened to you in the past year or two. Write an*
> *essay in which you relate this incident.*

Start Out

5
MIN

You've read many stories. You've also seen stories on TV and in the movies. You can use what you know about stories to help you to write your own story, or narrative essay. Give yourself five minutes to brainstorm and freewrite about each question below. If you run out of room, continue writing on a separate sheet of paper.

- **What** was the exciting thing that happened?

  _____

- **Who** are the people in the story?

  _____

- **Where** did the event take place?

  _____

- **When** did the exciting event take place?

  _____

- **How** did you feel before, during, and after the event?

  _____

- **Why** was the event important to you?

  _____

Put It Together

Use your ideas to decide on details for your story.

What: _____

_____

_____

Who: _____

_____

_____

Where: _____

_____

When: _____

_____

How: _____

_____

_____

Why: _____

_____

_____

Write Your Essay

Now you're ready to write your story. Use a separate sheet of paper. Remember that you want your story to interest your readers.

Look It Over

Read your story carefully. Ask yourself these questions:

- Did I include enough detail to describe the people and the places where the action takes place?

- Did I tell the events in a logical order?

- Did I tell why the event was exciting and important to me?

Think It Over

If any part of your story is unclear, how should you change it?
If possible, give your story to someone else to read. Have the person tell you what he or she likes best and what is unclear in your story.

"My teacher says I try to say too much for one essay. How can I decide which ideas to use and which not to use?" —Vida Melendez, 12

Here's a prompt that you might find on a writing test.

> *Describe what you would like your life to be like in the future.*

When you answer a prompt, you must limit your answer to what you can cover in a few paragraphs. A **cluster** can help you focus and limit your ideas.

Start Out

To make a **cluster**, write your topic and box it. Then write some parts related to your topic. To answer this prompt, you might choose home life, achievements, work, and possessions. Look at this cluster. Add your own ideas.

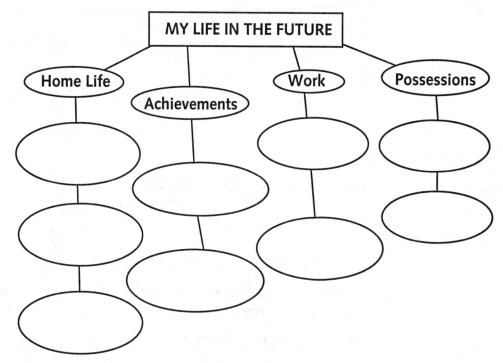

What overall thought or feeling do you have about your life in the future? Write a sentence about it. This will be the central idea of your essay.

_____

_____

Put It Together

Use details from your cluster to make an outline.

1. Write your central idea.

2. Use your cluster circles to decide on the main ideas for your supporting paragraphs. Remember you may have to leave out some ideas to keep your writing focused.

3. Think of details to use in your supporting paragraphs.

Central Idea: _____

Paragraph # 1 Main Idea : _____

_____

Supporting Details: _____

_____

_____

Paragraph # 2 Main Idea : _____

_____

Supporting Details: _____

_____

_____

Write Your Essay

Write your essay on a separate sheet of paper. Remember that you're describing important parts of your future life.

Look It Over

Read your essay carefully. Ask yourself these questions:

- Did I give a clear picture of my central idea?
- Are there any parts that I should leave out?

Think It Over

What was the hardest part of writing this essay? What would make it easier next time? Use the back of your essay to write your ideas.

How to Organize Information

"How can I tell which ideas to use and which ideas not to use?"
—Alfonso Tucker, 11

A prompt may ask you to write a short report. The prompt might give facts to use in your essay. Here's a prompt that you might find on a writing test.

> *Explain how weather forecasts are made. You can use these facts in your essay.*
>
> *—The National Weather Service uses radar to collect information about weather.*
> *—Radar can show a weather change hundreds of miles away.*
> *—The National Weather Service sends up 200 weather balloons every day.*
> *—Instruments in the balloons report weather conditions.*
> *—Instruments that float in the ocean send measurements of waves to satellites in space.*
> *—The instruments are in the Atlantic Ocean, the Pacific Ocean, and the Gulf of Mexico.*
> *—The satellites receive the information from the floating instruments.*
> *—Scientists get information from the satellites about the weather.*

Start Out

You can organize information by grouping related facts. For instance, you could organize the above facts into three subtopics: Using Radar, Using Weather Balloons, and Using Satellites and Instruments in the Ocean. Finish this chart.

Using Radar	Using Weather Balloons	Using Satellites and Instruments
To collect information	Instruments report weather conditions	Receive information from floating instruments

5 MIN

Put It Together

After you have grouped your facts, you can plan your essay. Use the following sentence as your central idea. *Scientists collect information about the weather in different ways.*

Now turn your three groups of facts into three supporting paragraphs.

Central Idea: _____

Paragraph # 1 Main Idea : _____

Supporting Details: _____

_____

_____

Paragraph # 2 Main Idea : _____

Supporting Details: _____

_____

_____

Paragraph # 3 Main Idea : _____

Supporting Details: _____

_____

_____

Write Your Essay

Write your essay on a separate sheet of paper. Remember, your goal is to explain how scientists collect information about weather.

Look It Over

Read your essay carefully. Ask yourself these questions:

- Does each paragraph in the body contain a main idea and details?
- Did I use the facts given in the prompt?

Think It Over

Show a friend your essay. Ask your friend if he or she understands your explanation.

Put Your Learning into Practice

Think about what you've learned in the last few lessons. Read the four prompts, choose one, and write an essay on your own.

Narrative

> You're sitting in the park when a bird drops a note at your feet. What does the note say? What happens next?

Persuasive

> In your opinion, why are video games good or not good for young people? Write a letter to parents to persuade them to agree with you on this subject.

Descriptive

> Describe a season of the year. Include sights, sounds, smells, and tastes. Describe how the season makes you feel.

Expository

> Teach your reader how to do something. (Here are some examples: shoot baskets, dress for a particular occasion, or babysit.) Be sure to include any tools and materials needed.

Start Out

Remember to relax, and to use the key words in the prompt you chose to help you. Use what you've learned about how to think of ideas, extend ideas, focus ideas, and organize information.

Put It Together

- Use an idea map, a cluster, brainstorming, or freewriting to come up with ideas and details to use in your essay.

- Put related details into groups. This organization will help you write and order your paragraphs. It will also help you write your central idea.

Write Your Essay

Write your essay on a separate sheet of paper. Use the notes you've made to help you write the introduction, body, and closing of your essay.

25 MIN

Look It Over

Review your essay. Read the questions below and put a check next to things you have done. Use these questions to help you see what parts of the essay you need to improve.

Narrative Essay

[ ] Did you describe the characters and tell when and where the events took place?

[ ] Did you support each main idea with details?

[ ] Did you put the events in a logical order?

Persuasive Essay

[ ] Did you write your opinion about video games in the introduction?

[ ] Did you include a main idea in each supporting paragraph?

[ ] Did you develop each of your ideas with reasons, examples, and facts?

Descriptive Essay

[ ] Did you use details to help your reader picture the season?

[ ] Did you omit any sentences that did not support your ideas?

[ ] Did you include your feelings about what you described?

Expository Essay

[ ] Did you present all the steps in the right order?

[ ] Did you leave out any steps?

[ ] Did you write sentences that are clear and easy to follow?

Think It Over

What is hardest for you about writing an essay? What can you do to make this problem easier next time? Write your ideas in a few sentences on a separate sheet of paper.

CHAPTER 2 STRATEGIES FOR CLEAR AND INTERESTING WRITING

This chapter will help you write clear and interesting essays. It will teach you how to connect your ideas. It will also show you how to use different kinds of sentences so that your writing will be more varied. These skills will help you improve your score on the writing test.

LESSON 1 How to Develop Good Transitions

A **transition** is a word or phrase that connects two ideas. A transition can tell your reader how two ideas are related. Look at this list of transitions, and notice how they link two ideas.

Check It Out

Transitions that show time order: *first, next, then, after, before, during, soon, finally, later*

Examples:

    a. Before his performance, Jason was nervous.

    b. During the game, the pitcher seemed tired.

Transitions that show how ideas are related or similar: *also, in addition, furthermore, similarly, for example, for instance*

Example:

    c. Smelly cigarette smoke annoys nonsmokers. **Furthermore**, it's dangerous to breathe.

Transitions that show how two ideas are not related or not similar: *but, however, on the other hand*

Example:

    d. The skater thought that he had given a fine performance. **However**, the judge did not agree.

Transitions that show cause and effect: *because, as a result, for this reason, therefore*

Example:

    e. We had a record amount of snow this winter. **Therefore**, we will have floods this spring.

Work It Out

Each of the following paragraphs has sentences that could be linked by a transition word or phrase. Fill in each numbered blank with a transition that fits the meaning.

Paragraph 1

The parade began with a marching band. **(1)** _____ , the mayor and an astronaut rode by in an open car. **(2)** _____ them came a float with a model of the space shuttle. **(3)** _____ , the next float carried scouts proudly holding the American flag.

(4) _____ , the parade came to an end. **(5)** _____ , a big carnival was held in Sherman Park.

Paragraph 2

Many animals use body language when they meet. **(1)** _____ , elephants wind their trunks together. Swans **(2)** _____ twine their necks together. **(3)** _____ , giraffes press their necks together.

(4) _____ , horses rub noses. Chimps, **(5)** _____ , touch hands to say hello.

Paragraph 3

The bedrooms in our house are quite different from one another. **(1)**_____ , my bedroom is small and cozy. **(2)** _____ , my sister's bedroom is huge. **(3)** _____ of this, the two of us sometimes talk about switching rooms for a couple of months.

(4) _____ , we never put this idea into action. The fact is that I love my bedroom too much to switch!

Look It Over

Read the paragraphs above with the transitions, then without them. On a separate sheet of paper, tell how the transitions make the meaning clearer for the reader. Give at least two examples.

How to Combine Sentences

When you write, try to vary the lengths of your sentences. If all your sentences are the same length, your writing can become boring. One way to avoid this problem is to **combine**, or join, sentences.

Check It Out

Here are some easy ways to combine sentences. Remember, however, that you should combine sentences only when they are related in some way.

Join short sentences.

Example:

    a. The hurricane blew the windows in. It knocked down trees. It caused the electricity to go off.

Correction:

    b. The hurricane blew the windows in**,** knocked down trees**, and** caused the electricity to go off.

In this example, the writer used commas and the transition word *and* to combine three short sentences into one longer sentence.

Sometimes you can put information from one sentence into another sentence.

Example:

    c. Nadine was extremely hungry. She hadn't eaten for twelve hours.

Correction:

    d. Nadine **hadn't eaten for twelve hours,** so she was extremely hungry.

Tie ideas together by using different transition words.

Example:

    e. My car broke down on a dark country road, and I felt scared. To get help, I walked to the nearest house and knocked on the door.

Correction:

    f. Because my car broke down on a dark country road, I felt scared. To get help, I walked to the nearest house and knocked on the door.

Notice that when you combine sentences, you sometimes have to change some of the words and the way you've ordered them.

Work It Out

Read the following sentences and circle the places where you could combine sentences. Then, rewrite the sentences in paragraphs on a separate sheet of paper. Make the ideas relate to each other more clearly.

1. Thunderstorms are scary. They bring lightning. They bring crashing booms of thunder.

2. A thunderstorm can change into a tornado. A tornado is even scarier.

3. Tornadoes always come from weather conditions that can cause thunderstorms. Not all thunderstorms lead to tornadoes.

4. A tornado forms from warm, wet air. The air rises from the ground during a thunderstorm.

5. The air starts to spin as it rises. It spins faster and faster. It touches the ground. It pulls things up with its high-speed wind.

6. Scientists have learned much about tornadoes. They have been studying them for many years.

7. The human eye can see only the part of a storm that is close. Radar can see the storm for many miles around.

8. In *The Wizard of Oz*, a tornado picks Dorothy's house up off the ground. The tornado sets it down in a strange land.

9. A real tornado causes great damage. It can blow off a roof. It can destroy a whole house.

Look It Over

Write two sentences with related ideas. Exchange them with those of a classmate. Combine each other's sentences.

How to Structure a Paragraph

When you write an essay, you put your thoughts in order. You do the same thing when you write a paragraph. In every paragraph, you should write the main idea in a **topic sentence**. In the other sentences in your paragraph, you can give **supporting details**. These details can be reasons, examples, and facts related to the main idea.

Check It Out

One way to structure a paragraph is to write the topic sentence first. The rest of the sentences in the paragraph should present your supporting details. Here's an example of a paragraph with the topic sentence in the beginning. The sentences that follow the topic sentence give **examples**.

> Many animals protect themselves by using venom, or poison, to kill or injure their enemies. Certain kinds of toads and spiders have glands that give off venom when they bite. Similarly, certain snakes use their fangs to inject venom into their enemies. Scorpions sting with their tails.

What details support the main idea?

_____

_____

_____

You can also begin a paragraph with supporting details and end with the topic sentence. This order is a good way to build the reader's interest before you actually state the main idea.

> A friend is someone you can trust with your secrets. A true friend will be on your side and keep your best interests in mind. If you're making a mistake, a friend will tell you the truth, even if it hurts. No wonder a good friend is hard to find. A good friend must have so many different qualities.

Write two or three details that support the main idea.

_____

_____

_____

_____

Work It Out

Read the following paragraphs and answer the questions after each one.

Paragraph 1

Many volcanoes rise from the ocean floor. For example, the Ring of Fire is a circle of volcanoes that rise from the Pacific Ocean floor. Mount Pinatubo in the Philippines is part of the Ring of Fire. Hawaii has Mauna Loa, the world's largest volcano. Mauna Loa also rises from the ocean floor.

1. Underline the topic sentence that gives the main idea.

2. Are the supporting details reasons, examples, or facts? Circle them.

Paragraph 2

In 1815, a volcano named Tambora, which is near the island of Bali in Indonesia, exploded. It killed 12,000 people on Bali and created a tidal wave that killed 80,000 more on nearby islands. Tambora also changed the weather around the world. There was no summer in 1815! Vesuvius, near Naples, Italy, erupted in Roman times and buried three towns. Another eruption killed 18,000 people. Volcanoes can be very dangerous and destructive.

1. Find and underline the topic sentence that gives the main idea.

2. Circle two sentences that support the main idea. Are the supporting details reasons, examples, or facts?

Look It Over

What is another way you could have ordered the topic sentence and supporting details in Paragraph 2? How would the meaning of the paragraph change? Write your ideas on the lines below.

_____

_____

_____

_____

_____

Put Your Learning into Practice

In this chapter, you learned how to make your writing clear and interesting. Now you can use what you know to write an essay. Read the prompts. Choose a different essay type than the one you chose in Chapter 1.

Persuasive

Pretend that you have a friend who is having trouble getting along with a sister or brother. Give your friend some advice on how to solve these problems. Write your essay in the form of a letter to your friend.

Narrative

Tell about a personal experience in which things didn't turn out the way you thought they would.

Descriptive

Describe what a perfect day would be like. Use details to help your reader see, hear, smell, feel, and possibly taste what the day is like.

Expository

Write about a hobby or interest that you have. Explain why you like it.

Start Out

5 MIN

Remember to relax. Underline the key words in the prompt you chose to help you think of ideas. Use brainstorming and some of the other strategies you've learned to think of ideas and details for your essay. On a separate sheet of paper, you may wish to make a chart, a cluster, or a web to organize your ideas.

_____

_____

_____

_____

_____

Put It Together

- Use transition words and phrases to show how ideas in sentences are related.

- Remember to vary your sentences. Combine sentences when you can.

- Check to see that each paragraph has a topic sentence.

Write Your Essay

Write your essay on a separate sheet of paper. Use your notes to help you write the introduction, body, and conclusion.

Look It Over

Read your essay carefully. Find the type of essay you wrote, and write a check mark next to the items that you are satisfied you accomplished in your essay.

Persuasive Essay

[ ] Did you state your opinion in the first paragraph?

[ ] Did you support your ideas with reasons and examples?

Narrative Essay

[ ] Did you describe the people in the essay? Did you tell where and when the action took place?

[ ] Did you put events in the correct order?

Descriptive Essay

[ ] Did you use details to help the reader see, hear, smell, feel, and taste the scene?

[ ] Did you describe your feelings about the scene?

Expository Essay

[ ] Did you include details to help the reader understand the topic?

[ ] Did you clearly explain why you enjoy the hobby or interest?

Think It Over

Now you know how to use transitions, combine sentences, and structure paragraphs. Which of these skills gives you the most trouble? How do you think you can improve your ability to use that skill? Write your ideas on a separate sheet of paper.

CHAPTER 3

MECHANICS AND USAGE

This chapter will give you some basic writing rules. Following these rules will help you improve your grade on a writing test.

Sentence Structure

A **sentence** is a group of words that **expresses a complete thought**.

Check It Out

A sentence contains a subject and a verb.

Example:

Subject Verb

a. A bird sang.

The **subject** is the person, place, thing, or idea that the sentence is about. The verb tells what the subject does or is.

Example:

Subject   Verb

b. The boy was running.

Subjects can be singular or plural.

A **singular subject** names one person, place, thing, or idea.
A **plural subject** names more than one person, place, thing, or idea.

Example:

Singular   Plural

c. bird   birds

Verbs can also be singular or plural.

Example:

Singular   Plural

d. sings   sing

When you use a singular subject in a sentence, use a singular verb. When you use a plural subject, use a plural verb.

Example:

Subject Verb

e. The birds sing in the trees.

Work It Out

A. Read each sentence. Underline the subject once. Underline the verb twice.

1. Summer is my favorite time of year.

2. People seem happier in the warm weather.

3. Tennis is my favorite summer sport.

4. I also enjoy basketball and baseball.

5. Sports are more fun in the summer.

6. My family spends time at a pleasant lake.

B. Read each sentence. Underline the correct verb.

1. We (is having, are having) a family picnic.

2. Relatives (arrive, arrives) from all over the state.

3. Each family (bring, brings) a dish to share.

4. Aunt Helen always (fix, fixes) barbecued chicken.

5. My brother Josh (do, does) magic tricks.

6. I hope the children (stay, stays) away from the poison ivy.

7. After lunch, everyone (relax, relaxes).

Look It Over

Look over your work. Did you have trouble identifying the subject or the verb in any sentence? On a separate sheet of paper, write one sentence with a singular subject and singular verb. Then write a sentence with a plural subject and plural verb. For each sentence, underline the subject once and the verb twice.

Sentence Fragments and Run-On Sentences

A **sentence fragment** is a group of words that does not express a complete thought. A **run-on sentence** is formed when two or more sentences are joined by only a comma or by words such as **and** or **so**.

This lesson shows you how to fix these mistakes.

Check It Out

A sentence fragment usually is missing either a subject or a verb.

Examples:

    a. Wanted to play soccer. (no subject)

    b. Keisha and her sister. (no verb)

A group of words can have a subject and a verb and still not express a complete thought. Such groups are also sentence fragments.

Example:

    c. Or Matthew speaks. (subject and verb but no complete thought)

You can fix sentence fragments by adding the missing subject or the missing verb. You can also fix sentence fragments by joining them or by making the fragment a part of another sentence.

Correction:

    d. Keisha and her sister wanted to play soccer.

    e. Keisha and her sister speak, **or Matthew speaks**.

A run-on sentence joins two or more sentences incorrectly.

Example:

    f. Five groups played at the concert, all of them were excellent.

    g. We finished our homework, we went to the playground.

To fix a run-on sentence, you can make two sentences.

Correction:

    h. Five groups played at the concert. All of them were excellent.

You can also rewrite the run-on sentence, using a transition word such as **after** or **because**. The transition word shows how the ideas are related.

Correction:

    i. After we finished our homework, we went to the playground.

Work It Out

After each example, write *sentence*, *sentence fragment*, or *run-on sentence* on the line provided.

1. Many young people in this country. _____

2. Studying the martial arts of Asia. _____

3. The martial arts are for self-defense, many people learn them as a sport. _____

4. Judo was the first martial art to be accepted at the Olympic Games, judo was accepted in 1964. _____

5. A judo contestant must throw the other person and pin the person on the mat, that's how you win. _____

6. In karate, both people attack, they can't touch each other.

   _____

7. Karate students wear colored belts, the colors tell what level the person has reached. _____

8. *Kung fu* is a form of fighting developed in China, it's also the name of a television series. _____

9. Strength, timing, and speed. _____

10. Learning how to react quickly to danger. _____

11. *Kung fu* has different forms, and some forms follow the movements of animals. _____

12. Leopard, tiger, snake, dragon, and crane. _____

13. Some historians think that martial arts. _____

14. Japanese martial arts are based on ideas from Zen Buddhism.

    _____

15. *Tae kwon do* is Korea's most popular martial art, it means "the art of kicking and punching." _____

Look It Over

Choose two of the sentence fragments and two of the run-on sentences that you found. Think of ways to make them correct sentences. Write your new sentences on a separate sheet of paper.

Adjectives and Adverbs

Adjectives and adverbs are words that are used to describe other words.

Check It Out

Adjectives describe nouns and pronouns.

Examples:

    a. We saw the **great, calm, blue-green** ocean.

    b. She seems **unhappy**.

    c. After the explosion, we helped the **lucky** few who escaped.

Adjectives answer these questions about nouns and pronouns:
Which one? What kind? How many? Whose is it?

Examples:

    d. I bought **this** car with a **big** motor.
       (Which car? What kind of motor?)

    e. I sat in **my** chair in front of **her** window.
       (Whose chair? Whose window?)

    f. The circus has **twenty** clowns.
       (How many clowns?)

Adverbs are words that often tell something about verbs.

Adverbs tell *how, when, where, or to what degree.*

Examples:

    g. He speaks **softly** and sings **well**.
       (Speaks how? Sings how?)

    h. She **usually** visits her friend Marsha.
       (Visits how often?)

    i. He thought **twice** about lending his tapes.
       (How many times?)

    j. Let's wait **outside**.
       (Wait where?)

    k. Finish your cereal **now**.
       (Finish when?)

Adverbs can also tell about an adjective or another adverb.

Examples:

    l. That was a **truly** great party!
       (How great a party?)

    m. They talked **very** loudly.
       (How loudly?)

Many adverbs end in *ly*.

Work It Out

A. Underline the adjectives in the sentences. Each sentence has at least one adjective.

1. I went to see my old neighborhood.

2. The street was different.

3. The man in the small local store remembered me.

4. I asked him what happened to my old building.

5. He told me that there had been a bad fire.

6. Twenty people escaped, but one person had a small injury.

7. This little gray cat escaped, too.

B. Underline the adverbs in the sentences. Each sentence has at least one adverb.

1. My report was finally complete.

2. We walked outside.

3. It was a very cold day.

4. We walked quickly because of the cold.

5. Mr. Johnson's dog was jumping happily.

6. The dog is often alone.

7. The dog's barks sometimes scare children.

Look It Over

Look over your work. On a separate sheet of paper, write two sentences of your own. Use adjectives and adverbs in your sentences.

Capitalization and End Punctuation

You know what capital letters are. You use one every time you begin to write your name. You probably also know and use the different punctuation marks for ending sentences.

Check It Out

Use a capital letter for the first word of a sentence.

Example:

    a. We are going to a basketball game tonight.

Use a capital letter for the first word of a direct quotation in dialogue.

Example:

    b. Carlos replied, "We'd like to go, but we can't."

Use a capital letter for the first and last word and the main words in the title of a book, story, play, poem, or song.

Example:

    c. I finished reading *A Tale of Two Cities* this afternoon.

Use a capital letter for the names of specific people, places, or things.

Examples:

    d. Liza Fanelli, Mayor Matsuda, President Jefferson

    e. Twenty-third Street, Oak Park, Atlantic Ocean

    f. Democratic Party, the American Revolution, Spanish

Use capital letters for the days of the week, months, and holidays.

Examples:

    g. Monday, January, Thanksgiving Day

Use different end punctuation for different kinds of sentences.

A statement or a polite command ends with a period.

Examples:

    h. This book is about World War I.

    i. Turn that video game off.

A question ends with a question mark.

Example:

    j. Have you read the book yet?

An expression of strong feeling ends with an exclamation point.

Example:

    k. What a great song that is!

Work It Out

A. Each of the sentences below has at least one mistake. Underline the letters that should be capitalized.

1. The teacher said, "the gettysburg address was written by president abraham lincoln."

2. it was delivered on november 19, 1863, to an audience in gettysburg, pennsylvania.

3. the speech was given during the civil war.

4. the war was fought to free the slaves and to keep the northern and southern states together as the united states.

B. Add end punctuation to each of the following sentences.

1. Have you ever heard of the Loch Ness monster

2. Loch Ness is a long and deep lake in Scotland

3. People call the monster Nessie

4. Nessie is believed to be a giant creature about 20 to 30 feet in length

5. Some people think it might be a dinosaur

6. Nobody has actually proved that Nessie really lives

7. What do you think

8. I'd hate to meet Nessie in the middle of the lake

Look It Over

Look over your work. Decide which rules you need to study more. On a separate sheet of paper, practice them by writing an example for each rule.

**Commas**

These rules will help you use commas correctly.

Check It Out

Use a comma to separate the city and the state in an address.

Examples:

    a. Sioux City, Iowa

    b. Little Neck, New York

Use a comma to separate the day and the year in a date.

Example:

    c. May 6, 1994

Use a comma after the greeting and the closing in a friendly letter.

    d. Dear Amanda**,**

The weather's great. I wish you were here.

    e. Love**,**

          Chris

Use a comma to separate words in a series.

Example:

    f. There haven't been any **thunderstorms, floods,** or **tornadoes.**

    g. We have McIntosh **apples,** Bartlett **pears,** and ripe **bananas.**

Use a comma after some introductory words or phrases.

Example:

    h. Yes, we have had several days of sunshine.

    i. After school, we rode our bikes to the park.

Use a comma to set off extra information that interrupts a sentence.

Examples:

    j. Michelle Goldman**, a rookie police officer,** made the arrest.

    k. The car**, of course,** was badly damaged.

Use a comma to set off a name used in direct address.

Example:

    l. Where are you going, **Dylan?**

Use a comma before the connecting word that combines two sentences.

Example:

    m. There was a cool breeze, **and** we were glad we brought jackets.

Work It Out

Add commas where they belong in the following sentences.
Each sentence is missing at least one.

1. Jack do you know what the homework assignment is?

2. Mix together flour baking powder sugar and salt.

3. Have you ever been to Los Angeles California?

4. My mother was born on April 26 1955.

5. My English teacher Mr. Washington was absent today.

6. Later that dark day our band was supposed to practice.

7. Art class is always fun but sometimes it can be messy.

8. Washing the dishes cleaning my room and taking out the trash are some of the chores I have to do every week.

9. Yes I did see that movie.

10. She bought her mother a birthday card and signed it: Love Jill.

11. That band comes from Seattle Washington.

12. The television doesn't work but we could listen to music.

13. The television broke down of course just as my favorite show was about to begin.

14. This year the national championship match will be held in Ann Arbor Michigan.

Look It Over

Look over your work. Which rules do you need to study more? On a separate sheet of paper, practice them by writing one example sentence for each rule.

Semicolons and Quotation Marks

This lesson will help you use semicolons and quotation marks.

Check It Out

Use a semicolon between two closely related sentences that do not have a connecting word.

Examples:

    a. It was time to leave; Luis grabbed his jacket.

    b. She thought she had made a mistake; she was wrong.

Use a semicolon before the words *however, therefore, nevertheless,* **and** *for example* **when they are used to connect two sentences.**

Examples:

    c. He says he is the only expert; **however,** I am also an expert.

    d. I did not know the answer to the question; **therefore,** I asked my older sister, Wanda.

(Put a semicolon before and a comma after the connecting word.)

Use a semicolon between items in a series that includes commas.

Examples:

    e. The winners of this award are **Chang Wen-jen, a dancer; Manuel Hernandez, a violinist; and Elise Lundstrom, a singer.**

    f. Henry wants to travel to **St. Louis, Missouri; San Francisco, California; and Vancouver, British Columbia.**

Use quotation marks around someone's exact words.

Examples:

    g. "I'd like to thank my teacher," said Wen-jen, "for all the help she's given me."

    h. The newspaper says, "Roads have a record number of potholes."

Use quotation marks around titles of articles, short stories, poems, essays, and songs.

Examples:

    i. She knows the poem **"Annabel Lee"** by Edgar Allan Poe.

    j. My favorite short story is **"Diamond As Big As The Ritz"** by F. Scott Fitzgerald.

    k. Billy's favorite song is **"Yellow Submarine"** by The Beatles.

Work It Out

A. Add semicolons where they are needed in the following sentences.

1. Dragons never existed however, they appear in tales and legends all over the world.

2. European dragons ate people Asian dragons helped people.

3. European dragons had huge wings and roared Asian dragons had no wings and made sounds like tinkling bells.

4. Some authors who have written books about dragons are Anne McCaffrey, who wrote *Dragonfight* and *Dragonsong* Laurence Yep, who wrote *Dragon Steel* and *Dragonwings* and Jane Yolen who wrote *Dragon's Blood* and *Dragon's Boy*.

5. There are no dragons on earth like these storybook dragons however, the Komodo dragon can grow to be about 10 feet long.

B. Add quotation marks and commas where they are needed in the following sentences.

1. Ari said I'd like to go back in time and slay dragons.

2. I could be a knight Ari continued and fight them.

3. It's too bad Ben replied that you're scared of horses.

4. That's not true his brother yelled. I could learn to ride!

5. Meet a young knight in the short story The Fifty-first Dragon.

Look It Over

Look over your work. Which uses of the semicolon and quotation marks gave you the most trouble? On a separate sheet of paper, write some sentences, following the rules that you had problems with.

7   Apostrophes

This lesson will teach you about the apostrophe (').

Check It Out

Use an apostrophe in a contraction to show letters are missing.

Example:

    a. Serena **hasn't** taken shop class yet.
       (The apostrophe replaces the *o* in not. **Has not = hasn't**)

Use an apostrophe in possessives to show ownership.

Examples:

    b. John Willams**'s** dog is running down the street.
       (The *'s* shows ownership.)

    c. The soldier**s'** boots were lined up in a row.
       (Soldiers is plural. Add an apostrophe to a plural ending in *s*.)

    d. My brother-in-law**'s** office is on Broadway.
       (Hyphenated possessive words have an *'s* at the end.)

    e. In the garage were Tony**'s** and Scott**'s** motorcycles.
       (Use *'s* for both words to show that both boys have motorcycles.)

Use an apostrophe to form the plurals of letters and numbers.

Examples:

    f. Hector got **90's** and **95's** on all his tests this semester.

    g. Mind your **p's** and **q's,** and you'll get along with everyone.

Do not use apostrophes with the possessive pronouns *hers, his, its, yours, ours,* **and** *theirs.*

Example:

    h. That book is **hers**. **Its** pages are torn.

Do not use apostrophes with plurals that are not possessive.

    i. The drama **students** put on **plays** for local **audiences**.

Be careful with words that sound the same.

Don't confuse *who's* **and** *whose* **or** *it's* **and** *its.*

Examples:

    j. **Who's** going to the party? (**Who's = who is or who has.**)

    k. **Whose** idea was that? (**Whose is a possessive pronoun.**)

    l. **It's** not yours! **Its** label proves that. (**It's = it is or it has. Its is the possessive form of the pronoun it.**)

Work It Out

Each of the sentences below has at least one mistake. Add apostrophes where they are needed. Cross out the apostrophes that don't belong. Change any word that is incorrect.

1. Most animals are raised by their mother's.

2. Some animal's fathers take care of the babies, too.

3. The eggs' of the Darwin frog hatch in the fathers mouth.

4. Theres a special pouch where the babies grow into tadpoles'.

5. When they become tiny frogs, they lose their tails and jump out of his' mouth.

6. Baby Emperor penguins owe much to their dad's, too.

7. These penguin fathers protect the eggs for 60 days in Antarcticas freezing weather.

8. Its amazing, but he doesnt eat at all during that time.

9. He wont leave the eggs until the mothers' come back to care for them.

10. Each mother penguin knows which of the newborn baby birds are her's.

11. Another baby bird, the rhea, gets it's food from the father.

12. A rhea is a large South American bird thats similar to an ostrich.

Look It Over

Look over your work. Which do you think is more difficult—using apostrophes to make contractions or to show possession? Write two examples for each on a separate sheet of paper.

One way to improve your spelling is to keep a list of words that you often misspell. Always refer to a dictionary. Look up each word, and add it, spelled correctly, to your list.

Check It Out

Here are some spelling rules you should know:

Words that end in *y* make their plurals in two ways. Look at the letter that comes before the *y* to see how to make the plural.

If a noun ends in a consonant and the letter *y*, change the *y* to *i* and add the letters *es* to make the plural.

Example:

   a. fly/flies, pony/ponies, berry/berries

If a noun ends in a vowel and the letter *y*, add the letter *s* to make the plural.

Example:

   b. bay/bays, day/days, donkey/donkeys

Sometimes, you will need to add the endings *-ing* or *-ed* to a word and double the final consonant.

Double the consonant if a word is one syllable and ends in a single vowel and consonant.

Examples:

   c. fan + ing = fanning   **d.** pat + ed = patted

Double the consonant if a word has more than one syllable and the accent is on the last syllable.

Examples:

   e. refer + ed = referred   **f.** control + ing = controlling

If the word does not have the accent on the last syllable, you generally do not double the consonant before adding an ending.

Examples:

   g. gallop + ed = galloped   **h.** open + ing = opening

Work It Out

A. For each sentence, write the correct plural of the word in parentheses on the line that follows the sentence.

1. The tour of three (city) went smoothly. _____

2. The mother dog cares for her four (puppy)._____

3. Sara found two (way) to walk to school. _____

4. One of the many (joy) of life is music. _____

5. The two (attorney) argued loudly. _____

6. The family of (monkey) chattered in the trees.

   _____

B. For each sentence, underline the correctly spelled word in parentheses.

1. In the heavy rain, Juan's vision was (limited, limitted).

2. Our parents (permited, permitted) us to go to the park.

3. The aftershocks are (occuring, occurring) hourly now.

4. Ms. Williams is (offering, offerring) to drive to the station.

5. The Tigers (defeated, defeatted) the Sharks in the play-off.

6. The best athletes will be (runing, running) in the race.

7. The debater (rebuted, rebutted) the argument effectively.

Look It Over

On a separate sheet of paper, begin a list of words that are hard for you to spell. Write the correct spelling of each word. Try to make up a rule to help you remember that spelling.

Put Your Learning Into Practice

Read the prompts below. Choose one to write an essay about. As you write your essay, keep in mind everything you've learned about sentence structure, capitalization, punctuation, and spelling.

Persuasive

> *Think about a rule at your school that you would like to see changed. State how you think it should be changed. Give reasons and examples to persuade the principal to make the change you suggest.*

Descriptive

> *Describe a person you would like to have as a friend. State why you feel that way. Give details to show the reader what this person would be like. This person can be someone you know, someone famous, or even someone completely imaginary.*

Narrative

> *Imagine you woke up one morning to find that you had turned into some kind of animal. Tell the story of that day. What kind of animal are you? What do you do? How do other people react to you in your new state?*

Expository

> *Peer pressure can be powerful. Explain how peer pressure works. Give your ideas about why you think people might be pushed into doing something they might not want to do. End your essay by saying how you think students can avoid feeling pressured.*

Start Out

Jot down some ideas about your answer to the prompt you chose. Use those ideas to come up with your central idea sentence.

_____

_____

Put It Together

- Be sure that your sentences express a complete thought.
- State the central idea in the first paragraph.
- Be sure each paragraph has one main idea.

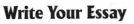

Write Your Essay

Write your essay on a separate sheet of paper. Use your notes to help you write your introduction, body, and closing.

Look It Over

When you have finished your essay, look it over carefully. Then use the checklist to see how you did.

Circle a number on the scoring scale after each question. (**5** is the highest you can score; **1** is the lowest.)

Does the essay clearly follow the prompt?

  1 2 3 4 5

Is the central idea stated in the first paragraph?

  1 2 3 4 5

Do all of the sentences relate to the central idea?

  1 2 3 4 5

Does the essay have important details, examples, or facts?

  1 2 3 4 5

Does the last paragraph restate your central idea?

  1 2 3 4 5

Check your sentences carefully. Does each one express a complete thought?

  1 2 3 4 5

Does each sentence begin with a capital letter?

  1 2 3 4 5

Does each sentence end with the correct punctuation mark?

  1 2 3 4 5

Think It Over

Of all the things you learned in this chapter, which do you think was the hardest? Review the rules that gave you the most trouble. Find one or two sentences in your essay that you think could be improved, and rewrite them on a separate sheet of paper.

CHAPTER 4 · REVISING AND PROOFREADING

After you've finished writing your essay, you can still make it better by revising and proofreading it. When you **revise**, you improve what you have written. When you **proofread**, you correct errors in spelling, capitalization, and punctuation. This chapter will help you learn how to revise and proofread your essay on a writing test.

LESSON 1 · Recognize Mistakes

Before you can revise mistakes in your writing, you have to find them. This lesson will help you learn what to look for as you read your essay.

Check It Out

Use this list as the main points to look for as you revise:

1. **Does each paragraph do its job?**
   The first paragraph should state your central idea. The paragraphs in the body of the essay should support your central idea. The closing paragraph should sum up your thoughts and state the central idea in different words.

2. **Does each paragraph contain a main idea and supporting details?**
   Detail sentences should add more information about the main idea sentence. Make sure each paragraph has this kind of focus. If you find a detail or idea that doesn't fit with the paragraph's main idea, cross it out or replace it with a detail or idea that supports the main idea.

3. **Does each sentence lead smoothly into the next sentence?**
   Transition words show how one thought is related to another. You can use transition words to connect two sentences. This will help the reader follow your thinking.

4. **Does each sentence have a subject and a verb?**
   Your essay should contain no sentence fragments. Look for sentences that do not express a complete thought.

5. **Does each sentence follow the rules of subject-verb agreement?**
A singular subject is followed by a singular verb. A plural subject is followed by a plural verb.

6. **Does the essay contain any run-on sentences?**
Run-on sentences are mistakes that occur when two sentences are connected with a comma. You can correct run-on sentences by adding a transition word or by changing the comma to a semi-colon or a period.

7. **Does the essay contain any sentences that could be combined?**
Sentences of the same length and structure can be combined to make them easier to read.

8. **Does the essay contain any capitalization, punctuation, or spelling mistakes?**
Your essay should contain no careless mistakes of spelling, punctuation, or capitalization.

Read the student paragraph below. Underline parts of the paragraph that you think need correction. Think about how you would correct each of these parts. Then read the corrected paragraph that follows. Did you identify each error correctly?

Draft

When Josie fixs a flat tire on her bike, she follows certain steps. First, she turns the bike over. So that the wheels stick up in the air. Then she pushes back the tire to see the bad tube. Next She pull the bad tube out. She puts the new tube around the rim and pushes it under the tire, she is sure to place the air valve in the hole in the rim. finally, she turns the bike upright and pumps air into the new tube.

Corrected Version

When Josie fixes a flat tire on her bike, she follows certain steps. First, she turns the bike over so that the wheels stick up in the air. Then she pushes back the tire to see the bad tube. Next she pulls the bad tube out. She puts the new tube around the rim and pushes it under the tire. She is sure to place the air valve in the hole in the rim. Finally, she turns the bike upright and pumps air into the new tube.

Work It Out

Carefully read each paragraph below, and think about how you would make it better. Underline each place where you think a correction is needed. Then write a revised version of the paragraph on the lines below.

1. Here's a way to find out how smart your dog. Show the dog a biscit or any other treat; than place the treat under an empty soup can. See how long it take the dog to figure out how to knock over the can and get the treat. smart breeds that do this quickly poodles and dobermans. I found my dog, which is a mutt, on the street.

_____

_____

_____

_____

_____

_____

_____

_____

_____

2. Amazon ants, which live in the western United states, need workers to survive. In fact, they raise other kinds of ants to be the workers, the Amazon ants steal the eggs of other kinds of aunts. When the eggs of the diferent ants are hatched, the Amazon ants capture them? The workers bring food, to the Amazon ants. Build their nests, too.

_____

_____

_____ _____

_____

_____

_____

_____

3. Radio still have many uses, even in the age of Television, we
use clock radios to wake us up. We lissten to the radio in our car.
Walking outdoors or exercising. We put on headphones and
listen to a Transistor Radio as we walks. also radios are importent
during emergencies. When power goes out, there is no TV? But
battery-operated radios can bring us infomation and help, when
we need it.

_____

_____

_____

_____

_____

_____

_____

_____

_____

_____

Look It Over

Review the list of important points to check when you revise. Reread
one of the paragraphs you just revised. Did you remember to check for
each point? How can you be sure that you will check for each point
when you revise on the essay test? Write a reminder to yourself.

_____

_____

_____

_____

_____

_____

LESSON 2

Decide Which Mistakes You Have Time to Fix

Remember that you need time to plan, write, and revise your essay. If you are given forty minutes, you should leave about ten minutes for revising and proofreading.

Check It Out

Here is a checklist of questions to ask yourself when you revise. The items are arranged from **most important** to **least important**.

When you read your essay, correct any mistakes you see right away. If you don't find mistakes, ask yourself questions from the checklist. Then read your essay again to see if there are mistakes you did not see.

- Does the essay answer the writing prompt?

- Is the central idea stated in the first paragraph?

- Does each paragraph in the body of the essay support the central idea?

- Does each paragraph in the body contain a main idea?

- Do the details in each paragraph support the main idea?

- Does each sentence have a simple subject and a verb?

- Are transition words used to connect related ideas and to combine sentences?

- Does the first word of each sentence begin with a capital letter?

- Does each sentence end with the correct punctuation mark?

- Are all the words spelled correctly?

- Are commas used correctly?

- Are specific names, places, and things capitalized?

Which of the mistakes listed above are you most likely to make? Which are you least likely to make? How does knowing your strong and weak points help you decide which items are most important to check for? Write your ideas below.

_____

_____

_____

_____

_____

Work It Out

Read the prompt and the persuasive essay that follows. Underline the parts of the essay that you think should be corrected. Identify and number the three or four points you think are the most important ones to fix. Then rewrite the essay on a separate sheet of paper.

> *Your town will vote on whether or not to use an empty building near your school for a student recreation center. Write an essay stating your opinion about this idea. Try to persuade your reader to agree with you.*

I've heard that our town might turn the building across the street from our school into a rekreation center. I would like to present the reasons why I support this idea.

The most important reason is that we need fun and time with friends after school. After being in class all day. Kids our age need to let loose." We need sports. We need fun activities like jimnastics, dancing, and arts and crafts.

There is no place like this place where teens can go. Most of us are stuck at home after school. We can go to the mall if a parent is home to drive us. Few of us are that lucky. There isn't much to do at the mall. A teen center would be more fun.

The building for the teen center is right across the road from the school. We can walk their easily. There is a big field for outdoor games. Because it is so close to school. School buses could take us home. If it is open until 7 P.M. most parents could pick their kids up after work.

I hope you will think about these arguments, and support this new use for an unused building. My friends and I would be willing to pitch in and help clean the building, paint and fix it up and bring equipment over, so would most teens in this town.

Look It Over

Look back at the essay you corrected. Did you need more time to find and correct mistakes? On a separate sheet of paper, write a few sentences explaining how you would use the time better if you could do this exercise over again.

Now you know what to look for when you revise and proofread an essay. You have also learned how to identify which points are the most important ones to correct. Now you can improve your skills by practicing revising and proofreading.

Check It Out

You can use what you've learned about revising and proofreading to improve descriptive, narrative, persuasive, or expository essays. You can improve your work by leaving time for revision and proofreading.

Work It Out

Read the following writing prompt and expository essay. Underline the places in the essay where you would make changes. Then rewrite the essay correctly on page 83.

What musical artists and groups do you enjoy? Explain your choices.

I have chosen two singers Janet Jackson and Domino and one rock group U.S.3 to write about. They all play different kinds of music that I enjoy.

Janet jackson is my favorite female singer. Because of her dancing. I really like watching her on music videos.

My two favorite songs of hers are Again and Because of Love. Again is a slow, sad love song. Because of Love sounds like a hip-hop song.

Domino is my favorite male singer. He dresses cool. Raps well, too. I like that he doesn't mumble like some rap singers. The rap song I like best is Sweet Potato Pie. I also like Ghetto Jam to dance to.

U.S.3 is my favorite group. I like the song Cantaloupe. I like the drumming. I play drums myself so I know. I also like the sounds of saksaphones and trumpets in the background. I want to play saks myself some day.

In conclusion, I would like to say that Janet Jackson, Domino, and U.S.3 are all top musical artists. I like some of their songs, such as Again, for their lyrics. I like some of their songs, such as Cantaloupe, for their instrumentals. And I like some of their songs, such as Ghetto Jam, for dancing. Of course, everyone has different tastes about music.

Rewrite the essay correctly.

_____

_____

_____

_____

_____

_____

_____

_____

_____

_____

_____

_____

_____

_____

_____

_____

_____

_____

_____

Look It Over

Look back at the draft and your revised copy of the essay. Think about the corrections or revisions that took the most time. Were they the most important revisions you could have made? On a separate sheet of paper, begin a list of the important revisions that take the most time to make.

Here's an outline of the key points in Unit 2. Choose the one point in each chapter that you find most helpful to you. Then, jot down words and phrases that tell the meaning of that point.

A. Planning Your Essay

1. How to Think of Ideas
2. How to Extend an Idea
3. How to Focus Your Ideas
4. How to Organize Information

_____

_____

_____

_____

B. Strategies for Clear and Interesting Writing

1. How to Develop Good Transitions
2. How to Combine Sentences
3. How to Structure a Paragraph

_____

_____

_____

_____

C. Mechanics and Usage

1. Sentence Structure, Sentence Fragments, and Run-on Sentences
2. Adjectives and Adverbs
3. Capitalization and Punctuation
4. Spelling Hints

_____

_____

_____

_____

D. Revising and Proofreading

Recognize Mistakes, and Decide Which You Have Time to Fix

_____

_____

_____

PREPARING TO TAKE THE WRITING TEST

What Is a Multiple-Choice Test?

Your writing test may have a multiple-choice section. You will be asked to answer a number of questions. You'll find four possible answers labeled Ⓐ, Ⓑ, Ⓒ, and Ⓓ. Only one of these choices is correct. Take a look at this example:

The word underlined below may be correct or incorrect. Choose the letter next to the correct form of the word.

1. The car that Becky is driving is <u>hers.</u>

   Ⓐ hers.   Ⓒ hers'.
   Ⓑ her's.   Ⓓ hers's.

The correct answer to this question is Ⓐ. You have to fill in the answer sheet to show the answer.

- Look for **1** on the answer sheet and fill in the space marked Ⓐ.
  Answer Sheet
  1. Ⓐ Ⓑ Ⓒ Ⓓ

Here are some helpful tips:

- Mark your answers on the answer sheet, or they won't count.
- Double check that you have placed your answer next to the correct item number on the answer sheet.
- Make answer marks dark enough to be read by the machine that scores the test. Each mark should fill the space completely.
- If you change your mind about an answer, erase the mark completely.
- Mark your answers on your answer sheet only.

Strategies for Answering Multiple-Choice Questions

Check It Out

Use the three strategies below to help you get a better grade on your test. They will help you avoid mistakes and save time as you take the test.

Strategy 1: Read the directions carefully.

Take a deep breath. Now, concentrate as you read the directions. You need to understand exactly what the directions tell you to do.

Look at this example:

One of the underlined parts in the following sentence is incorrect. Choose the answer that shows the incorrect word.

1. Unlike some other animals, <u>raccoons</u> always <u>chews</u> <u>their</u> food <u>thoroughly</u>.
   Ⓐ raccoons
   Ⓑ their
   Ⓒ thoroughly
   Ⓓ chews

The directions tell you that one of underlined parts is incorrect. Then the directions tell you to choose the answer that shows that incorrect word. Answers Ⓐ, Ⓑ, and Ⓒ show words that are correct in spelling and grammar. If you haven't read the directions carefully, you might choose one of these correct words.

Answer Ⓓ is correct.

Strategy 2: Read all the answer choices before choosing one. Identify wrong answers first. Then choose the right answer.

It is important to read all the answer choices before you choose and mark an answer. After you have read all the choices, see if you can identify any answers that you know are wrong. Eliminating wrong answers gives you a better chance of choosing the right answer.

Look at this example:

Read the paragraph below. Then choose the statement after the paragraph that best expresses its main idea.

2. Venus is the planet closest to Earth, but it's a lot different from our planet. Unlike Earth, Venus is surrounded by thick, yellow clouds.

This thick atmosphere is made up of carbon dioxide, nitrogen, and sulfuric acid. The atmosphere keeps the surface of Venus extremely hot—over 800 degrees Fahrenheit. Liquid water would just boil away on Venus. Nothing lives there.

Ⓐ Venus is the planet closest to Earth.

Ⓑ Only bacteria live there.

Ⓒ There is no water.

Ⓓ Venus is very different from Earth.

The directions tell you to choose the statement that best expresses the main idea of the paragraph. First, read all four answers. You can eliminate answer Ⓑ, because the paragraph states that nothing lives on Venus. Three answers remain. Answer Ⓐ is a true statement, but it is not the main idea of the paragraph. Instead, it is a detail. Answer Ⓒ is also a true statement, but it is not the main idea of the paragraph. This leaves answer Ⓓ. Answer Ⓓ expresses the main idea. Every other sentence in the paragraph backs up the idea that Venus is very different from Earth.

Answer Ⓓ is correct.

Strategy 3: Don't get stuck on one question. Make the best choice you can, then move on to the next question.

In a timed test, you will be graded on the number of right answers you give. For that reason, it's best not to spend too much time on any one question. Here is a way for you to figure out how much time you should spend on each question. First, find out the total number of questions on the multiple-choice part of the test. Then, divide the number of minutes you have to do the multiple-choice questions by the number of test questions. For example, if you must answer thirty questions during a sixty-minute test, you should spend no more than two minutes on each question.

Work It Out

Now, go back over the two examples above. Mark each answer clearly and correctly on the answer sheet your teacher has given you. Make sure the question number matches the number on the answer sheet.

Look It Over

Which strategy do you think will be most useful when you take the writing test? On a separate sheet of paper, write the tip and tell why you think it will be useful.

Practice a Multiple-Choice Test

Remember, taking a writing test is a skill like swimming or riding a bicycle. The more you practice, the better you'll become.

Check It Out

In this lesson, you will practice answering different types of multiple-choice questions. Your teacher will give you an answer sheet. Be careful as you mark it.

Work It Out

Give yourself fifteen minutes to answer the following questions.

Choose the words that best complete the new sentence. Don't change the meaning of the original sentence.

1. You can win as long as you believe in yourself.

    Rewrite this sentence, beginning with the words:

    If you believe in yourself,
    Ⓐ therefore you will win.
    Ⓑ you can win.
    Ⓒ furthermore you can win.
    Ⓓ yet you can win.

Choose the best way to combine the following pair of sentences into one sentence.

2. The class did an experiment. The class learned about magnets.
    Ⓐ The class did an experiment, and the class learned about magnets.
    Ⓑ The class did an experiment and learned about magnets.
    Ⓒ After the experiment, the class learned about magnets.
    Ⓓ The class did an experiment but learned about magnets.

Choose the best supporting detail for the underlined main idea.

3. I've learned a lot in science this year.
    Ⓐ Science is my favorite class.
    Ⓑ Now I know many facts about the solar system.
    Ⓒ I have science first period in the day.
    Ⓓ I also learned a lot in history and English.

Proofread this paragraph to find the error. Mark the letter that shows the incorrect word.

4. Last <u>monday</u>, we saw a fireworks display. It was a warm <u>summer</u> night. <u>There</u> <u>were</u> five hundred people watching the fireworks.

    Ⓐ monday

    Ⓑ summer

    Ⓒ There

    Ⓓ were

Choose the best supporting detail for the main idea expressed by the sentence below.

5. The prisoner made a bold escape.

    Ⓐ He was able to hide in a laundry truck going to the city.

    Ⓑ The prisoner was innocent.

    Ⓒ He had been in jail for two years.

    Ⓓ He didn't have a good lawyer.

The sentence below may be correct or incorrect. Choose the answer you believe is the correct form for the sentence.

6. Jack replied "I'm pitching today."

    Ⓐ Jack replied, "I'm pitching today."

    Ⓑ Jack replied "I'm pitching today.

    Ⓒ Jack replied I'm pitching today.

    Ⓓ "Jack replied" I'm pitching today.

Read the paragraph below. One of the underlined words is incorrect. Choose the answer that contains the right correction.

7. My <u>grandfather's</u> garden is full of <u>beautiful</u> flowers. He grows rose <u>bushes</u>, lilacs, daisies, and a dozen other plants. In the center of the garden <u>their</u> is a small pond.

    Ⓐ grandfathers

    Ⓑ beatiful

    Ⓒ bushs

    Ⓓ there

Look It Over

What problems did you have as you answered these questions? Look over the list of strategies from Lesson 1. Did you use each strategy to answer the questions in this exercise? On a separate sheet, write a few sentences telling how you might use these tips better the next time you practice.

Put Your Learning into Practice

Now you're ready to practice taking both parts of the writing test. Remember, read all directions carefully.

General Directions

You will write an essay on the prompt that is provided. You have thirty minutes to complete your essay. Spend the first few minutes thinking about the prompt and organizing your thoughts. You can make notes on a separate sheet of paper. Then, write your essay on a clean sheet of paper. Use a #2 pencil or a pen. Leave yourself a few minutes to revise and proofread your essay.

Essay Topic

> *In many states, music CDs and tapes must have warning labels on them. These labels tell parents if song lyrics are suitable for people under seventeen years old. Do you think that music products should be labeled this way? Tell why or why not.*

Multiple-Choice Portion

Now you will answer multiple-choice questions. Read the directions for each question carefully. Mark your answers on the answer sheet. Mark only one answer to each question. If you change an answer, be sure to erase your first choice. You may not know the answer to a question. Make the best choice and go on. You have twenty-five minutes.

Choose the best way to combine the following sentences.

1. We went swimming. We went horseback riding. We went hiking.
    - Ⓐ We went swimming, we went horseback riding, we went hiking.
    - Ⓑ Swimming and hiking and horseback riding.
    - Ⓒ We went swimming and horseback riding and hiking.
    - Ⓓ We went swimming, horseback riding, and hiking.

Read the paragraph. Choose the sentence that best expresses the main idea of the paragraph.

2. Many people enjoy watching sports events on TV. Some enjoy game shows in which contestants compete for money and prizes. Other viewers have favorite sit-coms that they watch each week. Soap opera fans watch their shows every day.
   - Ⓐ People enjoy different kinds of shows on TV.
   - Ⓑ Soap operas have the most fans.
   - Ⓒ Violence on TV is bad for you.
   - Ⓓ People watch too much TV in America.

Proofread these sentences to find the error. Mark the letter next to the word that needs to be corrected.

3. Chris and I does work at the mall. We are there each Tuesday.
   - Ⓐ does
   - Ⓑ are
   - Ⓒ there
   - Ⓓ Tuesday

Read the sentences below. One of the underlined words is incorrect. Choose the answer that contains the appropriate correction.

4. This year I am studying spanish. I am also learning about Mexico and other countries in South America.
   - Ⓐ Countries
   - Ⓑ Spanish
   - Ⓒ mexico
   - Ⓓ south America

Choose the best supporting detail for the main idea of this sentence.

5. There are many reasons that I like to read.
   - Ⓐ I learned to read when I was six years old.
   - Ⓑ My brother Danny reads more than I do.
   - Ⓒ I learn interesting things from reading books and magazines.
   - Ⓓ The library isn't far from my house.

Proofread the paragraph below to find the error. Mark the letter that shows where the error is located.

6. Roy my uncle is a track coach. He enjoys building things. Just last week, he built a playhouse for his children. Before that, he built a deck for his house.
   - Ⓐ Roy my uncle
   - Ⓑ enjoys
   - Ⓒ Just last week,
   - Ⓓ Before that,

The word underlined below may be correct or incorrect. Choose the letter next to the correct form of the word.

7. Is this football <u>yours</u>?

Ⓐ yours

Ⓑ your's

Ⓒ yours'

Ⓓ Yours

The sentence below may be correct or incorrect. Choose the answer that shows the correct form of the sentence.

8. "I'll call you later, Mindy said, after I get home."

Ⓐ "I'll call you later, Mindy said, after I get home."

Ⓑ I'll call you later Mindy said. After I get home.

Ⓒ "I'll call you later. Mindy said, after I get home."

Ⓓ "I'll call you later," Mindy said, "after I get home."

Read the paragraph below. Then write the letter of the sentence that doesn't belong in the paragraph.

9. We had a Middle Ages Day at school, and the whole class wore costumes from that time. **(A)** Many girls were dressed as princesses and other noble ladies. **(B)** My mother made my costume. **(C)** A few boys wore pointed hats with bells like jesters. **(D)** Most came as knights in armor, carrying swords.

Ⓐ A

Ⓑ B

Ⓒ C

Ⓓ D

The sentence below may be correct or incorrect. Choose the answer you believe is the correct form of the sentence.

10. Shawn read three books last month, he hopes to read another one during spring vacation.

Ⓐ Shawn reads three books last month, he hopes to read another one during spring vacation.

Ⓑ Shawn read three books last month, he hopes to read another one during spring vacation.

Ⓒ Shawn read three books last month. He hopes to read another one during spring vacation.

Ⓓ Shawn read three books last month, he hopes to read another one during Spring vacation.

Look It Over

As you look over the practice writing test you just finished, think about the questions below. Answering them will give you an idea of what kinds of things you need to practice.

The Essay

Look over your essay. Then use this scoring scale to grade your work.

Circle a number on the scale after each question. (**5** is the highest you can score; **1** is the lowest.)

Does the essay clearly answer the prompt?

1   2   3   4   5

Do the main ideas in the essay relate to your central idea?

1   2   3   4   5

Does the essay contain details that support the main ideas?

1   2   3   4   5

Is the essay organized in paragraphs that are clear and easy to follow?

1   2   3   4   5

Do your ideas flow smoothly from one to the other?

1   2   3   4   5

Did you make any errors in sentence structure, capitalization, or punctuation?

1   2   3   4   5

Now find out how you did on the multiple-choice questions.

The Multiple-Choice Questions

With your teacher, review any mistakes you made on the multiple-choice questions. Then make two lists on a separate sheet of paper. First list the questions that you got wrong. On the second list, write some ideas about how you can improve your performance.

Think It Over

What is the most important strategy that you will be able to take into the test with you? Why is this strategy so important for you? Write your thoughts in two or three sentences on a separate sheet of paper.

Here is an outline of the key strategies in Unit 3. Look over the whole outline. Then jot down your ideas about why it is important to use each strategy. These notes are just for you, so don't worry about writing complete sentences.

Strategies for Answering Multiple-Choice Questions

1. Read the directions carefully.

   _____

   _____

   _____

   _____

   _____

   _____

2. Read all the answer choices before choosing one. Identify wrong answers first. Then choose the right answer.

   _____

   _____

   _____

   _____

   _____

   _____

3. Don't get stuck on one question. Make the best choice you can, then move on to the next question.

   _____

   _____

   _____

   _____

   _____

A business letter has six parts.

1. **Heading:** your address and the date

2. **Inside address:** name and title of the individual you are writing; address of the company where that person works

3. **Salutation:** greeting and name of the person that you are writing

4. **Body:** your message

5. **Closing:** the closing greeting

6. **Signature:** your name

Here is an example of a business letter:

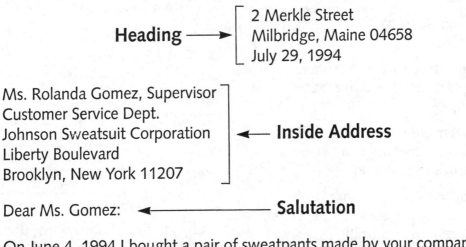

Heading ⟶
```
2 Merkle Street
Milbridge, Maine 04658
July 29, 1994
```

```
Ms. Rolanda Gomez, Supervisor
Customer Service Dept.
Johnson Sweatsuit Corporation      ⟵ Inside Address
Liberty Boulevard
Brooklyn, New York 11207
```

Dear Ms. Gomez: ⟵   **Salutation**

On June 4, 1994 I bought a pair of sweatpants made by your company. Three weeks later, I found a large hole at the bottom of the left leg. Please replace this pair of sweatpants as soon as possible. In this package, you will find the pants and a copy of my receipt.   ⟵ **Body**

Thank you for your help.

Closing ⟶ Yours truly,

Signature ⟶
Orlando Young

Adjective: words used to describe nouns or pronouns

Adverb: words used to describe verbs, adjectives, or other adverbs

Body: middle part of an essay

Central idea: most important idea of an essay

Closing: last paragraph of an essay

Descriptive essay: essay that describes a person, place, or thing

Detail web: a way to organize details

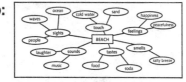

Essay: short piece of writing about a topic

Expository essay: essay that explains or gives information about a topic

Focus: element of good writing in which everything in an essay is about the central idea

Introduction: first paragraph of an essay; this paragraph states the central idea of the essay

Multiple-choice test: test that gives three or more answer choices

Narrative essay: essay that tells a story

Organization: ordering an essay to begin with the central idea, include supporting details, and conclude with the central idea

Persuasive essay: essay that states an opinion about an idea and tries to make the reader agree with that opinion

Plural subject: names more than one person, place, thing, or idea

Prompt: statement on a writing test that gives the writing topic

Revise: change an essay to improve it

Run-on sentence: two or more sentences joined incorrectly

Sentence: group of words that expresses a complete thought; a sentence contains a subject and a verb

Sentence fragment: group of words that does not express a complete thought

Singular subject: names one person, place, thing, or idea

Story map: a way to organize events and details

TOPIC
Central Idea
Details
Conclusion

Subject: the person, place, thing, or idea that a sentence is about

Support: main ideas and details that back up the central idea of an essay

Topic sentence: sentence that expresses the main idea of an essay

Transition: word or phrase that connects two ideas or sentences

Verb: word that tells what the subject of a sentence does or is